BOSTON

GALLERY BOOKS
An Imprint of W. H. Smith Publishers Inc.
112 Madison Avenue
New York City 10016

This edition first published in U.S.
in 1990 by Gallery Books,
an imprint of W.H. Smith Publishers, Inc.
112 Madison Avenue, New York, New York 10016

second printing

ISBN 0-8317-8825-9

Printed and bound in Spain

For rights information about the photographs in
this book please contact:

The Image Bank
111 Fifth Avenue, New York, NY 10003

Producer: Solomon M. Skolnick
Writer: Nancy Millichap Davies
Design Concept: Lesley Ehlers
Designer: Ann-Louise Lipman
Editor: Terri L. Hardin
Production: Valerie Zars
Photo Researcher: Edward Douglas
Assistant Photo Researcher: Robert Hale

Title page: *Reminders of conflicts in
the Republic's early years, the Bunker
Hill Monument and the U.S.S.
Constitution stand out against the
Boston horizon.* Opposite: *In this
aerial photograph from 7,000 feet,
Boston clusters compactly on its
peninsula.*

The waters of Boston Harbor, glazed
by low sun and dotted with boats
and Harbor islands. In the distance,
the city skyline.

History is a serious matter in Boston, even in its most whimsical forms. Take, for instance, the matter of ornaments atop buildings. It seems the stranger they are, the more affectionately Bostonians preserve them. Some date from colonial days, including Faneuil Hall's gold-plated grasshopper weathervane and the symbolic rivals of the Old State House, the lion and unicorn of the British Crown on one gable and the eagle and globe emblem of the U.S. on the opposite one. Others, like the gilded pine cone on the dome of the State House (emblem of the state's timber industry), recall the early days of Massachusetts statehood.

This page: *Boston Light, the nation's oldest lighthouse, on Little Brewster Island in Boston Harbor.* Below: *With the Common at their feet, downtown high-rises and the more modest towers of earlier years are set across a horizon of harbor and sky.* Opposite: *The 220-foot granite obelisk of the Bunker Hill Monument, erected in 1842 at Charlestown.*

This page: *"Old Ironsides,"* the nickname of frigate U.S.S. Constitution, *the oldest commissioned ship in the navy.* Below: *From 1799 to 1815, the* Constitution *emerged victor in 47 naval battles. The ship's bell was donated by descendants of the sailors who served on her.* Opposite: *The* Constitution *at permanent mooring in Charlestown. Public sentiment saved the ship from being scrapped, first in 1830 and again in the 1930's.*

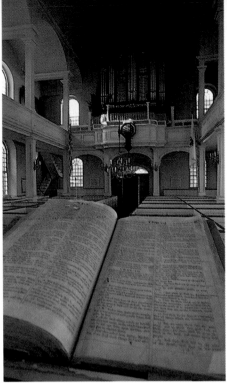

This page, left to right: *Lanterns atop an Old North Church staircase. In 1776, lights in its belfry warned patriots that redcoats were coming by sea. The interior of Old North Church. Built in 1723, it is the city's oldest church building. A view from the organ loft. The expansive east window, box pews, and raised pulpit with canopy suggest London churches of the period. Below: Paul Revere's statue backed by the steeple of Old North Church recalls his midnight ride. Opposite: Old North Church is at the northernmost point of the Freedom Trail in Boston's North End.*

Perhaps the figure Bostonians love best is the State House's "sacred cod" in the meeting place of the House of Representatives. Since pre-Revolutionary times the carved pine codfish has served as a reminder of the importance of cod fishing to the state's economy. The late nineteenth century also added a peculiar adornment to the downtown scene: the enormous teakettle that once advertised a tea merchant's premises. Although the shop which commissioned it disappeared decades ago, it still hangs on the front of a commercial building near Government Center.

Whether they look up, down, in from the waterfront, or out across the Charles, visitors to the Hub—as Boston has long been known—soon see evidence of events that took place in earlier centuries.

This page: *Paul Revere's house (1677) is the oldest dwelling extant in Boston. To its left stands the Pierce-Hichborn House (1711). In the background, Faneuil Hall. Beyond the Paul Revere house sign, an arched window ornaments a brick wall of the Pierce-Hichborn House. Light pours from Paul Revere's House by night. The overhanging second story is a feature typical of medieval English houses. Opposite: The Union Oyster House occupies brick rowhouses of the early 1700's. Daniel Webster sometimes patronized its horseshoe bar.*

Many of these events are common knowledge to most sixth graders, the rest relatively unfamiliar to anyone but Bostonians and their guests. Boston, very old as cities in the United States go, has a rich, complex past, much of which is literally intertwined with the present. Unlike urban areas such as New York where street layouts form tidy grids, Boston today still shows clear traces of the frontier settlement of 350 years ago in the village paths which are now major, if twisting, streets.

The first Europeans to make paths on the Shawmut Peninsula (which would later develop into Boston) were English Puritans, members of a reformist religious movement. The founders of the 1630 village had made the difficult sea journey to the New World in order to pursue the one interpretation of God's word they deemed correct.

This page: *A commercial landmark since 1873, this 227-gallon kettle once advertised a teashop. Beyond, the towers of the John F. Kennedy Federal Building.* Below: *Boston's New City Hall at Government Center, a prize-winning design completed in 1968, stands on the site of the earliest waterfront settlement.* Opposite: *The red, white and green colors of Italy's flag deck a stall in the produce market of the predominantly Italian North End.*

This page: *Architectural styles from French Empire to Art Deco combine in Suffolk County Court House (left, foreground) and its taller, newer addition (left, background).* (left, *Elizabeth Pain's headstone in King's Chapel Cemetery. Imprisoned for adultery, she may have been the model for Hester Prynne in* The Scarlet Letter. *Opposite:* Old City Hall, replaced as seat of Boston government in 1969, now contains offices and public agencies. Benjamin Franklin, in bronze, stands by its entrance.*

This page: *Layers of history. This 1873 cast-iron structure, former home of the* Boston Post, *occupies the site of the house in which Franklin was born in 1706.* Below: *The Old State House (1712–13) was the seat of the colonial government until the Revolution.* Opposite above, left to right: *Gold-plated American eagle and globe on the west face of the Old State House rival the British symbols at the other end of the building. The elegant tower, with its large windows and cupola, influenced the design of many other buildings in the colonies. Relic of colonial days, a muscular British lion adorns the east gable of the Old State House.* Below: *One-shot architectural history. Behind the Old State House tower, an ornate turn-of-the-century roofline and a vast façade of twentieth-century glass.*

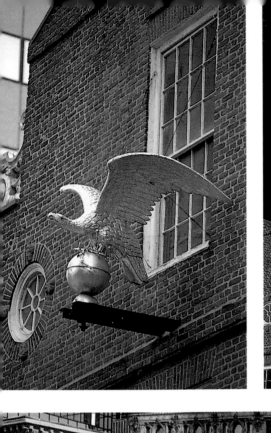

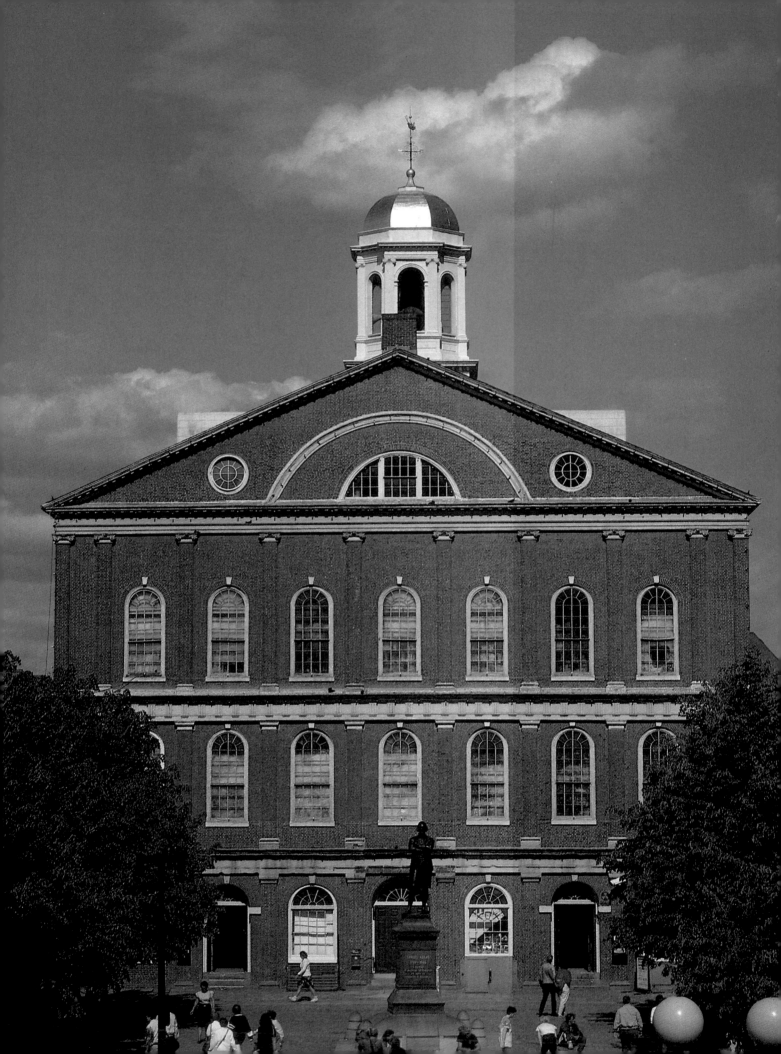

They could not altogether cast off their British heritage, as they demonstrated when they named the settlement Boston after the Lincolnshire home town of Lady Arabella Johnson and her husband Isaac, important early figures in the colony.

Puritan leaders controlled social and cultural life with a severity and lack of tolerance that can perhaps best be understood by reading Nathaniel Hawthorne's historical novel *The Scarlet Letter.* As the skull-and-wings carvings on tombstones in the old burial grounds downtown suggest, the focus of attention was on the corruption of this life and the hope of a purer world beyond the grave. In a society intent on rooting out sin wherever it sprouted, public disgrace of several kinds was the fate of those who did not hold with Puritan thinking—confinement in the stocks or pillory, branding on the hand, expulsion from the colony.

This page: *Faneuil Hall, built in 1742, draws its nickname "Cradle of Liberty" from the many important protest gatherings held here before the Revolution. Quincy Market interior. The reinterpretation of the old central produce market offers upscale wares as well as premium foodstuffs. Faneuil Hall's second-story assembly room is still used for public meetings. John F. Kennedy declared his candidacy for the Presidency here.* Opposite: *Venerable Faneuil Hall, fronted by a statue of Samuel Adams and topped by a gold-plated weathervane in the form of a grasshopper.*

Summer shoppers throng the tree-shaded pedestrian way between Quincy Market's south and central buildings. Below: In the foreground, the great copper dome of Quincy Market's central building. The North Market is beyond, bright with banners. Opposite: Quincy Market's three parallel buildings face the waterfront. The Custom House tower dominates the skyline behind them.

The 30-story Custom House Tower is a 1915 addition to an 1847 Greek Revival building. Once Boston's tallest structure, it remains a strong skyline presence. Below: Old Rowe's Wharf lies between bold contemporary buildings and their reflections in Boston Harbor. Opposite: The Custom House tower and the cupola of Faneuil Hall seem near neighbors in this telephoto shot.

This tugboat is now a restaurant, and the huge milk bottle a snack bar; their customers are visitors to the nearby site of the Boston Tea Party. Below: *Late sun gilds nineteenth-century warehouses along Summer Street.* Opposite: *In 1773, Bostonians disguised as Indians threw tea into the harbor from a ship like this to protest high taxes.* Overleaf: *Boston Common, open land since the city's earliest days, provides a 48-acre green space at the city's heart.*

Within a half-century, though, new and often non-Puritan settlers came, creating a less single-minded community. Boston was already becoming an important port, and port cities are seldom known as places of strict moral correctness. The sea provided the developing town with its vital links to Britain and, eventually, to the other young colonies along the eastern seaboard.

Apart from the street plan—or lack of plan—and the old graveyards, little physical evidence remains of the years of Puritan control in the seventeenth century. Eighteenth-century buildings like the Old State House and Faneuil Hall have been preserved, not only for their architectural interest but also because they were settings in a gripping national drama. Crucial events culminating in the American Revolution took place in and around Boston. Visitors can spend a day or more recalling those happenings by following a red-painted line along the city's sidewalks. Called the Freedom Trail, it marks out a path from one site to the next.

Some date the point of no return in the colonies' quarrels with Britain to the Boston Massacre of 1770. In that incident, five civilians died beneath the balcony of the Old State House when British soldiers, surrounded

by a mocking mob, opened fire. A circle of cobblestones marks the spot, a stop on the Freedom Trail. Another important step in the colonists' rebellion came in 1773 with the Tea Party. A daring band of colonists, resentful of the heavy taxes Parliament levied on imported goods, disguised themselves as Indians and boarded three newly arrived ships, emptying their cargo of tea into Boston Harbor. Visitors can now relive the symbolically important moment aboard a replica of one of the tea ships, the *Beaver*, moored near the historic site.

The Freedom Trail also passes beneath the roaring traffic lanes of the Central Artery into Boston's North End. The neighborhood of that name is itself a peninsula, attached to the rest of downtown Boston only by a narrow neck of land.

From the earliest days, North Enders have seen themselves as inhabitants of a separate town within a town. During recent centuries the North End has been home to various immigrant groups: first Irish (John F. Kennedy's mother grew up there), later Jewish, and most recently Italian. In the 1700's, it was a neighborhood of shopkeepers and craftsmen; among them was a silversmith named Paul Revere.

Park Street Church at the Common's northern boundary is a handsome 1809 landmark amid contemporary commercial structures. Below: John Hancock, Samuel Adams, Paul Revere, and many Bostonians less well known, lie in the Old Granary Burial Ground. Opposite: The finely proportioned spire of Park Street Church, 217 feet above Boston Common, points heavenward against the rich hues of sunset.

The Massachusetts State House, designed by Boston architect Charles Bulfinch and completed in 1798, stands at the top of Boston Common. Below: The gold leaf covering of the Massachusetts State House dome reflects sunset light in this west-facing view. Opposite: Early tombstones form neat rows in Old Granary Burial Ground, solemn under a coating of early snow.

Italian produce markets, bakeries, and restaurants tempt Freedom Trail travelers on their way to the oldest remaining dwelling in Boston, Paul Revere's house. From here he departed on his 1775 midnight ride to Lexington to warn the countryside of an approaching British company. After the Reveres' day, it was used as everything from an apartment building to a candy factory. The old place was in disrepair when history buffs organized to buy it in 1907 and restore it. Walking through the beam-ceilinged rooms with their diamond-paned windows and original furnishings, or standing beneath the deep gable that overhangs the front door, visitors momentarily capture a sense of the colonial town alive with fine craftsmanship.

Not far from the Revere House is another site of historical and architectural importance, Old North Church. Robert Newman, Revere's friend and the church's sexton, hung a pair of lanterns in its belfry to let militiamen across the river in Charlestown know that the British were approaching by sea.

Revere's ride and the skirmishes that followed brought more direct and violent confrontation between British troops charged with restoring order in the colony and colonists resolved to win

Banners in the State House's Hall of Flags honor Massachusetts regiments that fought in the Civil War and later conflicts. Below: Works of art, including a bust of Washington, ornament the semicircular Trustees' Room of the Boston Athenaeum, a private library. Opposite: From this marble hall in the Massachusetts State House, two staircases lead up to the chamber where the Commonwealth's senate meets.

Brick town houses of the 1830's and 1840's line Louisburg Square on Beacon Hill. At its center, a cast-iron fence sets off a rectangle of greenery. Below: Small town houses and old-fashioned street lights offer a quaint view of Old Boston on Beacon Hill's cobbled Acorn Street.

independence. The Battle of Bunker Hill in Charlestown was actually fought not on Bunker but on Breed's Hill. Early misreporting and confusion gave the battle the geographically incorrect name which has been used ever since. The British actually won, managing to drive the Americans out of Charlestown, but their high number of casualties encouraged the colonial troops because it showed that they could fight credibly against British regulars. Soon the British generals gave up the city as unrecoverable, and evacuated it. (Each year, on the anniversary of that day—March 17—Bostonians celebrate Evacuation Day.) As they departed, they burned Boston's lighthouse. That act of war demonstrated the crucial importance of the harbor to the well-being of the town—and to the entire colony.

The city's background of dependence on the sea partly explains Boston's loyalty to the nation's greatest symbol of the days of tall ships, the U. S. Frigate *Constitution*. Launched in 1797, she first saw action in 1801 during the conflict with the Barbary pirates. Later, when Britain and its former colonies faced off again in the War of 1812, the *Constitution* won victory after victory. During one of the many naval battles of those years, legend has it, the ship got the nickname "Old Ironsides" when an enemy cannonball failed to pierce the sturdy oak hull. Upon seeing this, one of the crew cried out, "Her sides are made of iron!" By 1830, though, the day of ships like the *Constitution* had passed, and she was scheduled for the scrap heap. Roused by Oliver Wendell Holmes' poem "Old Ironsides," the people of Boston objected so vigorously that the ship was instead restored. After another overhaul in the 1930's, the vessel was sailed to all the ports of the U.S. so that those who had given money for the restoration could come aboard and see the results. Today she is towed across the harbor and back once a year on the Fourth of July to turn her around at her mooring so that she will weather evenly. Horns sound all over Boston Harbor as other ships salute the oldest commissioned vessel.

In the years that followed the *Constitution's* days as a warship, Boston was being transformed from a colonial port to a proud cultural and intellectual center for all New England. Charles Bulfinch, the great architect of these years, designed the State House to stand on a commanding height above the Common. His plan featured the pillars and dome of the classical style, looking back to the traditions of democratic Greece and republican Rome that shaped the public life of the new nation in so many ways. Bulfinch and his

Horizontal afternoon light picks out the patterns of cast-iron ornament and shutter slats on the upper stories of Beacon Hill house fronts. Below: *Distinctive silhouettes against a glowing evening sky, Beacon Hill bow-fronts and spires line the way to Storrow Drive and the Charles River.*

The Hatch Memorial Shell, summer home of the Boston Pops, and where the Orchestra performs each July, anchors this panorama of Beacon Hill and the skyline beyond. Right: A much-loved figure, Arthur Fiedler is memorialized in this sculpture, which is located not far from were he conducted Boston Pops concerts for 50 summers. Opposite: Vistas of Beacon Hill brick and contemporary towers rise behind the Longfellow Bridge of 1908, the oldest surviving span linking Boston to Cambridge.

followers were also much involved in the building boom on Beacon Hill behind the State House, where wealthy merchants and political figures in the fledgling Commonwealth government were raising their houses.

A prosperous trading center like Boston needed a new waterfront marketplace. Faneuil Hall, the respected old assembly room and market of the colonial period, was too small for the needs of the growing city, even after the addition of a new third story. Progressive Josiah Quincy was the mayor who worked to have the Town Dock filled in to provide additional wharfside space. What is now known as Quincy Market was built on the reclaimed land. Its 512-foot central market building under an oval dome and the flanking warehouses of North and South Market opened in 1826. They were extensively renovated in the 1970's and continue as a thriving center of Boston commerce, with up to 50,000 visitors a day.

Pedal-powered swan boats, each carrying up to 20 passengers, have glided along the Public Garden's pond since 1877. Formal flowerbeds, geometric paths, specimen trees, and a small pond combine to make the Public Garden a relaxing midtown retreat. The suspension bridge above the Public Garden's pond, overhung by a willow coming into leaf. Bright flowers and shrubs deck the pathways. Opposite: An 1869 bronze statue of George Washington in the Public Garden.

Cultural institutions also sprang up throughout the city in the post-Revolutionary years. In 1803, a group interested in literature formed the Anthology Club. The organization published the country's first literary magazine and founded the Boston Athenaeum as a private library. Members of the public are welcome to tour the institution's 1849 building on Beacon Street, which houses a distinguished collection of art works and rare books.

City towers provide constant evidence of urban life just beyond the green oasis of the Public Garden. Below: *Boston old and new: The brownstone spire of Arlington Street Church rises behind Public Garden trees and in front of contemporary high rises.* Opposite: *Paintings line the richly carved stairway of the Ames-Webster House in the Back Bay, a showpiece of Victorian elegance.* Preceding pages: *Swan boats at day's end.*

Clouds of magnolia blossoms hide Back Bay doorways. Bay and bow windows on upper stories give each town house an individual character. Below: June's floral abundance crowds front gardens on Commonwealth Avenue, where the spacious town houses date from the late 1800's.

Throughout the nineteenth century, the U.S. publishing industry and the authors who provided its materials were Boston-based more often than not. Nathaniel Hawthorne, one of the country's first great writers, enjoyed strolling through King's Chapel Burying Ground, the city's oldest cemetery, and found inspiration there for his historical fiction. Louisa May Alcott, whose *Little Women* remains a classic for young readers, and novelist William Dean Howells both lived briefly on Louisburg Square. Essayists Ralph Waldo Emerson and Henry David Thoreau, both active in the most important intellectual movements of the time, had ties to Boston. William Lloyd Garrison began his campaign against slavery at the Park Street Church. Another Boston abolitionist, Julia Ward Howe, wrote "The Battle Hymn of the Republic." Henry Wadsworth Longfellow, author of "Paul Revere's Ride," was so well known and loved a poet that the bridge by which he often crossed from Cambridge into Boston was renamed in his honor.

In the mid-nineteenth century, city planners of the crowded peninsula again turned to extending the limited land area available for building. This time they filled in the marshy region known then—and now—as the Back

Behind profiles of Trinity Church saints, windows of the nearby Hancock Building reflect one of Trinity's three towers. Below: Church spires rise up from the largely residential Back Bay (foreground) and Beacon Street neighborhoods.

Bay, using gravel brought by train from Needham. The vast engineering project, begun in 1857, took 43 years to complete.

Builders, eager for the opportunity to lay out straight streets at last, followed closely on the heels of the landfill contractors. They created Commonwealth Avenue and the other wide boulevards which were the height of urban style at the time and lined them with stately houses and hotels. The Back Bay became the smartest residential district in the city, a fitting locale for the great religious building of the period, Trinity Church at Copley Square.

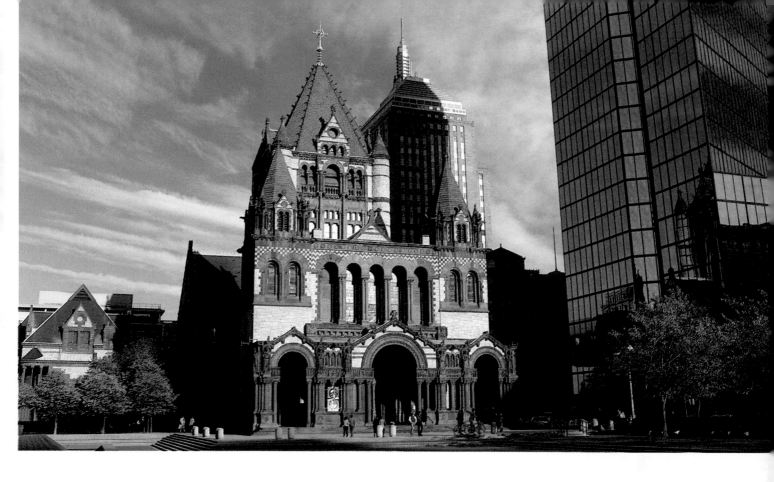

In Copley Square, masterwork of
architect H. H. Richardson, Trinity
Church is flanked by Hancock
buildings, old and new. Below:
Wrought-iron chandeliers and gates
guard an entrance to Boston Public
Library. In the background at right
stands New Old South Church.
Opposite: Postmodern design
includes traditional details in the
New England Building on Back
Bay's Boylston Street.

In recent years, with urban households shrinking and center-city property values soaring, the Back Bay's roomy town houses have in most cases been divided into apartments and condominiums. The neighborhood is home to an increasing number of commercial structures on a grand scale. They include the Prudential Tower, standing huge and square amid its plazas, and the 60-story John Hancock Tower, an I. M. Pei design completed in 1976. Large glass sheets held in place with black aluminum frames that visually blend into the façade form its exterior surface. They make each plane of the building a vast mirror that reflects both neighboring buildings and the changing light. At 790 feet, the Hancock is the tallest building in New England.

The 52-story Prudential Tower, faced with green glass, rises amid the open plazas of the Prudential Center complex. Below: A diagonal camera angle provides a novel twist to this view of Donald Delue's sculpture "Quest Eternal," backed by the Prudential Tower. Opposite: The Christian Science Church, the mother church of the faith established by Mary Baker Eddy in 1882.

In the years of the Back Bay's gradual transformation from marshland to chic residential quarter, Bostonians recognized the need to create additional parkland within their rapidly expanding city. The tradition of "green space" at the city's center had long ago been established by the Boston Common, a feature of the downtown landscape since the days when the earliest Bay colonists used it as a militia training ground and pasture. The Common had grown more parklike since the Bulfinch State House and

The courtyard of the Isabella Stewart Gardner Museum. The 1902 structure incorporates sections of Italian buildings collected by its founder. Below: Tiers of Venetian balconies rise above the Gardner's central courtyard. Its plantings are changed to reflect the season.

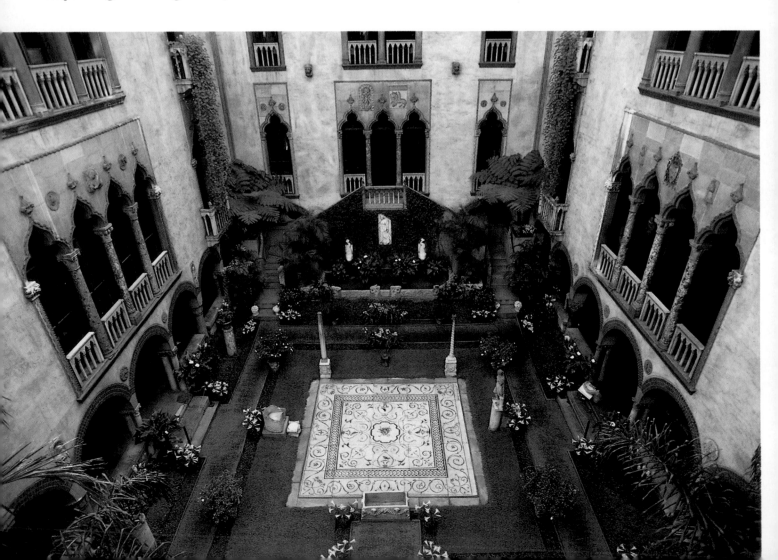

rows of elegant town houses had been built around its edges. One of the first reclaimed areas of the Back Bay, located just beyond the Common, headed the list of the new parks as the Public Garden. While Bostonians enjoy the Garden's memorial statues and its formal floral plantings, they reserve a special affection for the swan boats that cruise its lake from spring to fall.

The parks commission, created in 1875, made a very wise decision in 1878: they

Roses and pool in Fenway Gardens, a link in the "Emerald Necklace" of parkland that winds inland from the Charles River. Below: A sellout crowd packs Fenway Park for a Red Sox game, upholding the city's tradition of wildly enthusiastic support for all its sports teams.

Arnold Arboretum, a botanical garden that is part of the Emerald Necklace. Six thousand species of trees and shrubs thrive in its 260 acres. Below: Snow coats peninsular Castle Island and Fort Independence, a nineteenth-century stone fortification built to protect the Boston Harbor channel. Opposite: The John F. Kennedy Library at Columbia Point, designed by I.M. Pei, houses the President's papers and memorabilia. Preceding page: The Dorchester Heights Monument celebrates a Revolutionary victory: Gunfire from the site influenced the British decision to evacuate Boston in March 1776.

brought in Frederick Law Olmsted, the landscape architect who had designed New York's Central Park, as an adviser. Olmsted and the commissioners worked together to develop a grand plan for an "Emerald Necklace," which would circle the greater downtown area with parkland. The system that resulted from this ambitious plan includes six major parks and the parkways connecting them, in all a continuous green stretch nine miles long. Among the parks are the Arnold Arboretum, a botanical garden administered by Harvard University, and the Charles River Reservation — the Esplanade — a slender strip of parkland along the Boston side of the river. Views of the Cambridge skyline and sailing craft on the Charles make it a favorite of the city's walkers and joggers.

From the other side of the Charles, Cambridge's towers give it the look of a place older than Boston itself. In fact, settlement in the two cities began about the same time, in 1630. The Puritans, far from the English universities where their clergymen had been trained, founded a ministerial training college in Cambridge, with 12 students starting classes in 1636. It survives today as America's oldest institution of higher learning, Harvard College. The first three printing presses in the colonies were also set up in Cambridge.

The Rogers Building at the Massachusetts Institute of Technology in Cambridge houses its School of Architecture and Planning. Below: *The quadrangular plan of Harvard and its proximity to the Charles River are apparent in this aerial view.* Opposite: *The domed towers of Harvard's buildings add charm to the Cambridge skyline.*

Harvard, and intellectual life generally, are still in many ways at the heart of Cambridge life. The city is also home to one of the country's most distinguished technical institutions, the Massachusetts Institute of Technology. Overall, the Boston area has the highest concentration of colleges and universities in the U.S.

Boston is arguably the nation's most historically important city. By far the largest urban area in New England, it is home to institutions as revered and diverse as the U.S.S. *Constitution,* the Red Sox, and Harvard. Each of its neighborhoods retains a strong individual character,

This page: *Entrance to the Fogg Museum, Harvard's fine arts museum. The yard in front of Lowell House, one of three "New Houses" built in the 1930's in the Colonial style of earlier Harvard buildings. Shade trees and sun-dappled walks— quintessential Harvard.*

Ivy in autumn hues clothes the multicolored brickwork of Memorial Hall, built to honor Harvard men who died in the Civil War. Below: Light radiates from the Widener Library, sharply defining the 12-foot Corinthian columns of its portico. Overleaf: On the Charles River, college crews train in the early-morning sunlight.

from the tidy brick alleys of Beacon Hill to the Victorian grandeur of the Back Bay and from the Italian North End to the large-scale apartment and office towers that increasingly dominate the waterfront. Wherever Boston visitors turn, they will be aware of a city that has always had the good luck, over its three centuries of habitation, to find among its citizens concerned people of vision. These Bostonians have not only recognized the need for change but also have determinedly preserved unique and irreplaceable evidence of the city's past—as well as the nation's. Today's thriving, livable city is their just reward.

Index of Photography

All photographs courtesy of The Image Bank,
except those listed, "Stockphotos, Inc."